A Narc free World

AF208141

Calvina Braganza

 pencil

ISBN 978-93-5610-865-3
© Calvina Braganza 2022
Published in India 2022 by Pencil

A brand of
One Point Six Technologies Pvt. Ltd.
123, Building J2, Shram Seva Premises,
Wadala Truck Terminal, Wadala (E)
Mumbai 400037, Maharashtra, INDIA
E connect@thepencilapp.com
W www.thepencilapp.com

Author biography

This book is written personally by me, a woman from a very big ancestral Royal family. It briefly states about my personality and how it was formed from my early childhood through traumatic experiences. As I recalled my memories as I grew up as a beautiful adult. The book is titled as" A Narc free World" because of my dysfunctional upbringing and wrong parenting. Narcissism prevailing in my early caregivers as a result of my Self-doubting nature. This book elaborates on how I bravely broke the chains of codependency as a truly strong empowered woman of High Standards and Self-worth thereby breaking the chains of toxicity. I am now a creative artist, writer, anchor and a talented handcrafter. So knowledgeable that I have a lot to share to the world. This book is telling all the struggles and the stories of my life.

CONTENTS

Acknowledgements

I would like to dedicate this book to my mother Betty and my sister Dolvyn and in memory of my late Godmother Blazie as a tribute and sincere gratitude for being there as strong pillars in my tough times that I battled in hard times, a moral support with strong principles and values.

Introduction

The knowledge from this book is very authentic and genuinely helpful for all people recovering from mental and emotional abuse and turmoil. It is a representation of my own experiences as to how I dealt with torture of my upbringing as an innocent little child. The stories that punctured my heart and the cries of my past wounded bruised inner child. Right since birth and childhood upbringing upto adolescence all my old bitter memories that have faded away. Depicting the law of mirroring as to why I was a family scapegoat and seen as a problem child. The stories of my adulthood that drives me out of sanity. As the people exclaim gazing sarcastically "look, She's the crazy one." "Oh, see who is bipolar". Right from Getting bullied in school by classmates and peers , excluded outside frienships circles and the list goes on. In the latter chapters with exercises details and guidance of inner work and to reconnect with oneself and heal past wounts. Everything is mentioned very meticulously in details for almost anyone recovering from emotional and mental abuse or stress.

The birth of a first child

After waiting eight long years, the Lord heard everyone's prayers and the news of my birth, a sense of joy in everyone's hearts. A ceaserian baby so pure white as a snow white complexion. The doctor published upon the newspaper titled "Mr and Mrs Braganza family long awaited arrival of a baby girl after 8 long years in Dr Rebello hospital" The immense joy of my parents after my birth. On the baptism day all relatives were there to carry, play and cuddle a cute little pie all day. Dozen of servants allotted each task of the house were assigned given extra duties with the new born child. My mother was living a codependent pattern in her relationships with people pleasing habits. My needs were not being met in healthy ways. That's all what she passed on to me. She was having narcissistic traits too . She was controlling, resentful, having a victim mindset and was pessimistic.

Early Childhood years

I had experienced intense gaslighting especially amongst public. She would accuse me of the things I would not do nor did and would plant seeds of doubt in my mind through her guilt tripping and would simply find faults in me when it wasn't at all my fault. Thereby violating my boundaries and I grew up as a very timid and shy person. My Godfather was a very arrogant man and my mother dumped me along with my sister at his house for quite many years. Ever since the age of five I was kept there and he was very loud and boastfully talkative man with a big ego. Such a drunkard mad family that I used to always doubt myself and question myself like as though it was all my fault. Seeds of hatred and anger were planted that began with my trauma. I had no voice whatsoever, so full of fear of everyone and those around me. My mother was unjust and devalued all my achievements, though I was born clever. And I excelled at all academics that I failed to express myself. My emotional vulnerability were at its peak. I was screaming from the inside out suffocating from within. No one was willing to lend a ear to listen.

Begining of trauma

At home my parents were physically away from me and emotionally detached and no any justifications done whatsoever.

I was a little headless chicken walking on eggshells. Yet I can't forget those abusive words penetrating my heart and piercing my Soul. A feeling of inadequacy and thoughts about me screaming "I am not good enough". Being compared to the other cousins, put downs, being yelled at with insulting words like bastard, idiot etc

Comparisons with my sister and the list went on eroding my self worth. In that narcissistic family none were spared. All were succumbed helplessly to cope in the unhealthy dynamic. As my Godfather was the omnipotent, grandiose, malignant, overt and abusive parent to his own children and my sister and me. My godmother that is his wife was an empath, extremely people pleaser fending for everyone's needs, playing a role of a good samaritan. She was so social and giving to the poor and the needy. Her selfless service was her motto without keeping her own best interests at heart. She too was a victim of blame game where none were spared.

Upbringing of the children

My cousins that were his children were golden children and I was Scapegoated along with my sister who was an invisible child along with me. We all were headed to please the greater narcissist, Our Godpa. The house was a real drama stage with the absence of Godliness. In fact there were night outs, parties, discos, picnics and outings. They hosted TV shows along with us kids with all adult content with obscene vulgar movies. And I felt shy about talking about it to anyone. My parents Relationship was quite good with my Godparents that kept their bond strong. She was so gullible that she could easily get drawn to their schemes and manipulation tactics. She never stood up for herself though she was mistreated by them just like us. I was a keen observer and many times I noticed his superficial charm, lightening rage, thunderous loud voice, unreasonable jealousy which was a pathological envy. He couldn't stand to see his own family members achievements. He would minimize my accomplishments and under-rate them. And only brag about himself and his wife to everyone in public. He was a very vindictive and judgemental, hot tempered man. He gave and set a bad example for his children through faulty parenting. Very selfish and ego-centric person was he. My sister and myself had to face indifferences and comparisons, were put up ina pressure of competition and I was belittled, humbled down.

Home life at relatives place

My grades were very excellent at school. Yet I was put down. I was stressed out even at the dinner table. My opinions didn't matter after all it was my relatives home, not my home. The feelings of being abandoned from my parents arms and away from my irresponsible caregivers, to dump me and my sister at my relatives place. We were two vulnerable helpless children kept in their hands and had to bear all the injustice and be puppets at their hands. The house was a dungeon filled with morons who laughed at the expenses of us. All we had left to do was to cry helplessly with embarrassment and shame. Godpa had the full authority and command over all of us. He was very arrogant and would never accept no for an answer. He absolutely lacked in empathy and had a very fragile ego. Seeing his arrogance people got intimidated by his behaviour and insulting words. Sometimes he would unreasonably lash out in anger and scold them for no reason. This shame was projected on all of us children living in his house.

School days

In school I was a shy and timid person as a result of slowly damaging and gradually eroding my self esteem. I could constantly doubt myself. I was the most vulnerable victim of bullying and would come at home with all the other childrens and peer groups complaints. Hitting, slapping, ragging classmates. Competition on the rise, a demand for excellence at its peak. Injustice and partial treatments and teachers favouritism was too much to bear, some kind of nonsense happening there. My mother had completely neglected my needs and my sister and I was at the Godparents mercy. They were our caregivers. It was a feeling as though I lost my parents at an early age and a sense of been given away for adoption. Inspite of having parents at home who are living till today. All these deeply buried feelings of loneliness due to abandonment caused at a tender young age. I even started to attract toxic unhealthy and selfish friends who would not care for my well-being and would not respect my boundaries.

Relationship with my mother

My mother never respected my personal boundaries. She would guilt trip me each and everytime I would say no. She is a very pessimistic woman with a victim mentality. And no matter how much I do for her was never enough. She would take all the credit of my hard work and success and if any minor incident by chance a mistake would happen or occur by me; she would spare no room for criticism and would absolutely blame me for everything. I saw many narcissistic traits in her. She absolutely lacked in empathy in my early childhood years. I had to put myself last and accept all her opinions and put her on a pedestal as a top priority by forgetting all my needs. So much of self sacrifice at a tender age. I was given a chance in High School for a theatre workshop and was playing the role of a of a queen. I had to literally back off and give the role to another girl not just because I had no costumes and my mother was neglectful about my needs and the costumes I was supposed to arrange to wear for the play. She was least bothered. She deprived me of many things I could ever remember. A very bitter and punitive person, would show no remorse towards us and treated us very badly. Thereby planting seeds of doubt in our minds.

Upbringing at parents home

My mother would compare me with other kids and say "see, how well behaved and neatly they are dressed, you cannot even be nor do half of what they do", constant criticisms and I would go out of balance, thinking to myself as to how should I please her. But all my efforts went down in vain she made it damn sure that anything and no matter how much I do will never be good enough for her. She was so we'll bonded with my God parents. She adores them and would be well bonded and in good books with narcissistic people. Sometimes I would wonder why She gets attracted to all sorts of toxic and evil people.

Environment at relatives place

As far as I would recollect many times I saw my Godfather getting triggered in jealousy. He had a demon inside him, whenever he would see someone happy he couldn't stand it, that he would fly into outburst of rage and lash out. Sometimes he would compare me with other cousins and my sister to devalue me. He said very nice good things in comparison with me and my cousins making me feel poor of myself thereby belittling me. He would oppress people at the cost of his wife. Wife would go on pleasing all the people and do service to the poor and needy and he would take all the credit of her selfless service. Other people were obliged to pay visit to their home, so he would gain admiration, respect, service and other forms of narcissistic supply at his wife's expense. He would then brag out loud and insult, demean and sometimes even sarcastically used putdowns upon those innocent people.

Painfull childhood

My Godfathers children grew up very bitter, hateful and resentful. I used to very often wonder why such knots would form in my stomach amongst such toxic selfish people. That I had a sense of weak boundaries and a poor sense of self worth. So many years of my life I lived in fear. A habit of people pleasing developed in me, due to my parental upbringing. My mother was the main person to influence it in me. In my relationships with colleagues, friends everywhere I would get pushed by people and did not know how to stand up for myself when mistreated. I was even walked over like a rug, shamed and scolded apparently for no reason at all, as a result amounting to sadness and loneliness. I would feel so lost and lonely even in a crowd, that it would hurt me deeply from within. I was living everyday in fear, saying to myself "what would people think about me" thereby doubting and questioning myself. Questioning myself saying "Do those people like me?" This was an inner-gaslight. My inner critic was narrating that I was constantly questioning my own reality harshly thereby doubting myself, my sanity. In actual reality it was not at all my fault.

Challenges growing up

Outside in toxic environments many times I came across cunning people who would plan, plot and come with bad intentions. I really didn't know how to figure them out, that they turn so nasty, insideous like jackals. Deep within my heart and soul cried out loud that I need a worthy meaningful life. My needs were not been met. My absolutely selfish narcissistic mother on her own confusions would just punish me and would not allow any form of freedom. I didn't know how to fight back for the love that I needed. I still crave and long for her love. In my early childhood upto adulthood the bonding from my parents were missing. I missed the love that I needed. I was abandoned, rejected, dismissed, betrayed. Many times my mother gaslighted me in public unexpectedly as though she didn't trust me. This is how I disconnected from her. That deep sense of shame buried inside me made me to curse her calling her a witch, devil. I used to cry out her name's in outburst of anger and frustration but the end result all went in vain.

Life in adolescence

When in adolescence I reached to college at the age of 18. I was diagnosed chronic Bipolar personality disorder. That changed my personality and I was kept under observation. I was hospitalized and given strong drugs as medication. The doctors told my mother that the medicines will be lifelong. She cried out loud. As there was no remedy. I would chase behind emotionally unavailable partners and would attract all toxic men. And would wonder why as I was deprived of love from my mother when I needed it the most. Many people found out seeing my weird behaviour. In school other children played silly pranks on me and went on till college and youth too. Joking, sarcasm, mockery kept happening and went on. School days were aweful, life sucks kind of story.

Too much disciplinarians were those nuns, very strict English medium girls school competition everywhere. A struggle to be perfectionist. The girls were all quiet sensitive and turning psychologically and mentally disturbed children. I could sense it in their behaviour and interpersonal relationships.

Growing up in school days

There were no boys in our school and yet inspite of all this, speaking to or even about boys was considered an offense and was punishable. So much was I living in fear amongst those neurotic nuns. Thrown out of the class, accused falsely by other children's crimes and caught and punished wrongly blamed in the victim game most of the time. They just got away with their mischievous pranks, and I used to get caught and punished for it. There was hell of a price to pay in school. College time there was a relapse too, a huge one. Oh no, thought it was coed, I was not happy there. There was politics going on there. Oh, how I hated it. Teachers were very partial and mean in giving marks for the students. Favouritism was being played. I was labelled as a clown of the class in High School. Teachers were also great bullies and would punish the students very harshly. I could sense the injustice going on there.

Academics and performance at School

I was the best singer in school and the whole class applauded listening to my beautiful songs I was the best dancer in school winning many prices for competitions and was known as the best ranking in the entire School scoring very good grades, passing in good marks and coming with flying colours all teachers would like me because of my cleverness and good performance even my mother praise me for all my results. I was a very mischievous child too, and the captains in charge would refuse to believe it that it was me. I was given the priviledge to hoist the flag in red house team for march past in spite of not being the captain as it was all because of my loud and powerful voice. God has blessed me so many gifts and talents and it was little challenge to share it with the world ,as they were all in finite. In the field of music, arts and crafts I excelled . I would rank 8th in the entire class of sixty students. And my mother would be very proud of me that she would praise about me to the other parents.

Neighborhood and external environment

I many times noticed my neighbours behave in a very mean and hostile manner towards me. They would envy me so much, and my sister too was not spared in this story. She too had taken a lot of back stabs, insults, injustice etc. along with me. In other words our childhood was very traumatic and full of pain that we had to compete against each other to show our worth. She too was very intelligent. In school the competition was very unhealthy, politics amongst nuns and amongst students thereby Injustice prevailing everywhere. We had to keep up to the name of our school. The teachers never put any effort in training but our parents had to take up the burden to groom us. Many times I was treated poorly and was deprived of my mother's love and affection that I needed the most. This resentment got gathered inside built up into self-hate. As I would constantly doubt myself and found myself in socially anxious situations that I didn't know how to preserve my own sacred space, not knowing that I was lacking in boundaries. As a result of me being walked over by others, being regarded as a pushover thereby being treated as a doormat. I would then sit with the grudges later many at times getting worried about asserting myself and not knowing how to stand up for myself.

Relationships with people

In later years I attracted a lot of toxic people situations relationships constantly living in fear and not knowing how to protect myself from evil, selfish people and energy vampires wrecking my poor soul, not knowing how to protect my self and my precious energy that I gave in too much even when not needed that I lost myself in that process. I couldn't stand aggressive drunked men and their insults as it was rooted in my childhood trauma starting from my Godfather I was falling victim of negativity and toxic vibes given by the people falling in such a pathetic situations of high conflict, so great was the trauma bond as a result of low self esteem and so great was the darkness in me beginning with shame, very often do I look back at my miserable past and I recollect my old memories of sadness and loneliness in the emptiness within sounds kind of a weird fantasy that I too would fall for evil, cunning and selfish people who would undermine my worth.

Challenges faced and struggles

Many times I came across people that would trample over me, walking over me stripping away the little that I had with me leaving me empty and shattered. All they would only want from me and give nothing back in return and by chance give only misery and pain. I understand that they too were wounded and bitter people. In many co-incidents was I mistreated being Scapegoated and deprived of the love that I needed. I lost temper on people taking me for granted especially at home. Many peers, toxic friends in my surroundings tried to teach me a lesson by throwing me out of my own circle thereby sabotaging my freedom isolating me away from good people. I used to many at times feel very hurt from within. A deep sense of grief buried inside of me. My own uncle molested me twice and when I told my mother she refused to believe and didn't take action, as a matter of fact she pleased him with gifts because he's a family. So much was the injustice. People would label and call me names. Many times I would easily get fooled by others due to my innocence and co-incidents like these would re-occur. Neither did I have the guts to fight back that I lost my innocence.

A fight back struggle

As I lost my inner-voice that was demanding boldness to stand up for myself for what is right I lost my innocence as I grew up I developed a lot of bitterness, resentment and hatred towards my mothers partial treatment and faulty parenting. She was an over indulgent parent. I even became an agressive person and would pick fights even with strangers. So much were the demons of rage in me that I couldn't stand people who would violate my boundaries. So impulsive and wreck less in my speech and behaviour towards people even at home. Many at times I made a Fool out of myself. As it went on I started to have malicious humour at the expense of others and my jokes were of a deadpan of a variety and neither would I care if it would hurt the sentiments of people around me. I was a laughing stock everywhere but at the same time I had a strong core identity not to get carried away by other people's opinions. So knowledgeable that I knew what decisions to make for myself for my own good and empowerment.

Coping strategies

I would very often enjoy quiet time alone in solitude to recharge my drained energy. I preferred being alone as the energies of people, surroundings would affect me, because of my sensitive nature I could pick energies of people. Very often I would attract toxic, manipulative people and didn't know how to protect my energy from them. At times I too would behave like them, just to mirror their actions and teach them a good lesson. I couldn't stand control freaks and no wonder would often encounter them. This would seriously drive me insane. Shouting, yelling calling out names. I was labelled in society as a fighter cock due to my conniving nature and would pick fights even with strangers. Thereby attracting a lot of narcissistic people and toxic people in my life. Very often I found myself in high conflict situations due to my weak boundaries. Thereby experiencing a series of gaslights.

Workplace environment

In many workplaces I took up jobs that were all dysfunctional with unethical work environment having employers showing no remorse towards the mistreatment of the workers and co-workers in my surroundings that were so toxic . I was put up in a complete fight and flight situation and was constantly walking on eggshells. A victim of blame and dominance and also was subjected to workplace bullying. I had to do all odd jobs and run errands and work below my dignity taking up the responsibility of irresponsible co-workers and firings of the bosses. Taking all kinds of mistreatment, being poorly paid or getting fired in a series of workplaces. I was labelled as a good for nothing in society. The rate of being compared to my sister due to my poor performance was quite high as a result of thereby leaving me upset , resentful and furious.

Social Anxiety and challenges

I was not accepted in fact was getting rejected everywhere in almost all social circles. From being excluded saying "odd one out". Sometimes publicly humiliated or embarrassed by peers for acting wires being labelled as a clown. Slowly as the years progressed I realised that they all were symptoms of PTSD. As a result of occurrence of my childhood unresolved past trauma. The main root cause was because I denied, suppressed, repressed and disowned my emotional wounds. It was simply very difficult to sit down with my emotions in silence by contemplation sounding so impossible to journal it down or simply sit and meditate and come up with solution. Very frustrating to even relax in it as a result of my split personality. I was a chameleon amonst people, faking to make it. I was prepared to act and become a different person in order to be accepted and validated. It was so very difficult for me to forgive those from my past and I had a lot of resentment and pent up anger in me. The rage burning would trigger me so badly that I had to take medications to numb it. Being in a crowded place would drain me leaving me exhausted emotionally. That was the reason I would take alone time lasting on a couch to recharge and balance my list energy. From birth was I so sensitive to loud noises, thunder, smells , energies of people and allergic to coffee, alcohol and stimulants and was born delicate being fussy with food.

Voyage in the midst of challenges

I was very fond of music and art as it was my passion. Whenever I felt mentally disturbed listening music would soothe my Soul. As I grew up in later years I had a good appetite for food and clothing. I was and still the person who would wear branded , trendy and fashionable clothes. This would mark a high self-confidence and a sense of self worth. Daily mundane routine would bore me to the core and I would keep changing jobs as a result get dissappointed in my career. One fine day I came across a priest and he guided me strictly that I need to love myself. I laughed at him and took it as a joke brushing it off. He also told me that I needed to shut my mouth because of my excessive talking. I had questioned authorities and disrespected them for their unexpected, unethical work environment and mistreatment towards other co-workers and subordinates. In many incidences I appeared rude and dominant in society. I was too loud and boisterous in fact for quiet many years. After so long did I finally discover as it was during the pandemic that I needed to discover my soul purpose . I often drifted away searching from places to places, relationships after another, changing jobs multiple times, but never content with it. There was a burning desire that I will become a creative fashion designer as I was very talented in many arts and crafts, stitching clothes as I had done my tailoring courses in government institutes and my grandmother was feeling proud of me. She too was a tailor cum fashion designer.

Life at home with its own colours and beauty

My grandmother was very innovative in designing her own clothes and she created a lot of handicrafts during that time. She was a strong, confident and empowered woman quiet modern in her thinking even dressing style. My Grandpa was a freedom fighter, and being brought up in a Royal family we were granted many priviledge. I was blessed to live in a huge portuguese Architectural house with a big garden view in my compound and lovely greens in the backyard kitchen garden with herbs and spices etc. My neighbours were quiet quarrelsome but my mother knew how to maintain peace and integrity amongst those hostile people. My Godfather had a lot of greed for the share of the house and would express his lust for our property by manipulating his wife that ie. my godmother. She too was walking on eggshells and didn't put him in his place. And would enable him inspite of him being wrong and unjust. I would suppress all these resentful feelings and bitterness. Very often I would ask my mother why don't you speak up for what is right. But her response would always be Shutup, you will never know when you will need their help. This misery and pain grew up more and as I grew up with sadness, loneliness and emptiness within.

Lessons learned through tests and trials

As I encountered many damaged people in my life, setting boundaries was very crucial though I had a trouble in doing so, I would find myself in troublesome or quarrelsome situations most of the time as a result of me attracting toxic and high conflict people. It was It was difficult to say no but get persuaded and swayed by the opinions of others. This would make me very frustrated and many at times I would lash out yelling at the top of my voice. Slowly as the year passed by, I found out the bliss of self-love and establishing my own personal truth with setting up boundaries and I realised the value and importance of it through the struggles of my past. Gatekeeping was crucial by all means especially when dealing with toxic people as I would keep attracting narcissistic people most of the time. The challenges and lessons I learned in life made me a very strong person.

Effective Gatekeeping near toxic people

The first time someone attacks your space and the moment a person gaslights you, please address it and call it off. When you make excuses, justify and enable their behaviour. Even inspite of you telling them that they simply bothered you with their bad behaviour or mistreatment don't give excuses for their actions. Whatever your reason is watch them and do your own deep dive by trusting your gut in making your own decisions. Pay attention to your sensations what your gut is telling you, especially when it doesn't feel right. Our inner child wounds are responsible for our rationalizing voices. Don't confuse love over abuse, it's called trauma bond. Watch over these patterns as red flags as they have a series vicious cycle that begins with love bomb into future faking, devalue, abuse, discard, chaos, isolation , invalidation, breadcrumbing etc. and the cycle repeats in these series of patterns. Be cautious as to not giving into the magical feelings and ideas that illusional seen, heard, understood as that they rationalise the excuses to keep the so called "magic show" to distract you from illusions. There is no reality in it and it's all fake. It's going to be very toxic, so that's why it's fast, move in, vacations, family married everything very fast. For every one of your stories there started with something too fast. The quicker you move faster the more chances are to get devalued The sooner they have you locked up the more they can control you. So they keep continuously harrassing you by constantly texting and calling showing their needy nature and react badly when you don't respond back. They come out very arrogant and dangerous and think you are lucky to be in a relationship with or married to them. Like as though they did you a favour. Quite ego-tistical in nature and when you miss those red flags they ignore you, and the cycle begins. Make sure you turn on your mind when you're gaslighted . The best thing is to say goodbye by holding on to your reality and communicate when respect is granted in doing so. Or else turn it off.

Gatekeeping for shielding oneself

While dealing with toxic people turn on your mind when you are been gaslighted best thing is to say goodbye. Hold on to your reality and communicate if respect is granted and only if needed so, or else turn it off and leave the person or situation and move on. It will heal on its own. Staying in the relationship will destabilize you and impair you in long-term. The future faking is a classic love bombing technique and if they come to know your goals and dreams they will cleverly knit your dreams with that of theirs by fake promising. You will end up waiting for a lifetime. Be careful of making overly big sacrifices, giving up on your goals to make them happy. Soulmate and TwinFlames are all a blunder created with their faking. Better to stay safe at home with isolation or with family and loved ones. You don't have to sacrifice the things that are important to you. As they ask you to give up even basic things. Be bold early on in a relationship and get out of it immediately. Fear, guilt and shame even ego keeps you stuck in the traumabonded relationship. Only the worthy should be allowed to be with you in your life. Kick out the toxic people as a good means of gatekeeping. Shut the voices of other people that plant the seeds of doubt in your mind before it grows up. Remember that you cannot let people who gaslight and manipulate you cannot be let in to determine your self -worth. Walk away and gently slam the door against such unhealthy people.

Karma for toxic people

Just as the famous saying goes "every dog has his day" each an every person has his karma. Plant the seeds of love, gratitude, trust and it gets added upon you. When you plant the seeds of hatred, anger and despair you get the same on return and it all comes multiplying at some point in your life. I have seen a lot of these toxic people living double lives through their evil intentions, lies, hatred and malice. Their endings were quite ugly. They usually get abandoned in their old age or commit suicide or live a pathetic and miserable life. In their old age there is none to call their own and give them a decent burial, not even a hand to hold at their death bed. Because as they age and get old they get more unbearable and no one can stand them to tolerate their nonsense. They look unattractive and loose all their charm. All those people who were once their enablers refuse to go back to them as they know how evil and hazardous it is to go to them and find it challenging to tolerate their nonsense. They all slowly drift away even their children refuse to see them. Their significant other leaves them through legal notice and children's custody stating that it's unsafe for them and their children. They live and die all alone, isolated abandoned in a miserable state with none to call their own. Such a great dreadful miserable and bad karma. All the years that were planted on bad soil is what they reap their harvest and get rewarded for their bad actions.

How to deal with gaslighting

How to respond when being gaslighted:

i. Turn to loved ones, avoidance of isolation is must and seek out emotional support with the help of family.

ii. Take notes: Recording events immediately after the incident happens provides evidence you dont need to second guess yourself. Jotting down highlights from a conversation or using a smartphone app to record your argument offers something to review when your memory is called into question. You may not feel comfortable confronting the person, but your notes can help you recognize what's happening.

iii. Set clear boundaries: Establishing boundaries can interrupt someone's attempts to gaslight you and provide some physical and emotional space.

The next time it happens, you might say:

Δ Excuse me! It seems we remember things differently

Δ If you continue like this, I don't want to talk to you anymore

Δ We can talk about it, but if you shout I'm going to leave

Δ Hold on to the things that make you who you are. Practice self-care in solidarity, do relaxation techniques. Meet your physical and emotional needs, also surround yourself amongst healthy, normal, cheerful and nurturing people who will celebrate and uplift your Soul.

Δ Name and address any doubts and fears around your

Self-worth
Δ Work through painful or unwanted emotions
Δ Accept that you didn't cause or deserve gaslighting
Δ Explore and set healthy boundaries
Δ Navigate attempted manipulation
Δ Manage stress
Δ Handle conflict productively.

Exercises for Self-care

Why do you not take better care of yourself?

Δ Write down the reasons you deprive yourself in practicing self-care.

Δ What beliefs do you have about your right to take care of yourself

Δ List all the ways that you deprive yourself of nurturing, support, protection and so forth

Δ Make a list of the needs you are meeting and how you are meeting them

Δ List the needs that have gone unmet and think of ways that you can begin to meet them

Exercises to check in your body

i. Look in the mirror and notice what expression you have on your face. does your face look angry? sad? afraid?

ii. Now sit down and take a few deep breaths

iii. Check in with your body what emotion is being expressed there? If there is heaviness in you chest what emotion might that be? If there is an uneasiness in your stomach, what that might be saying about how you are feeling?

iv. Notice any tension in your body in your shoulders, your neck, your jaw, your stomach, your hands

v. Take a few more deep breaths and ask yourself what emotions are connected to this tension. Is it anger? Fear? Sadness?

vi. Now, taking the information you have gathered from the expressions of your emotions on your face and the tension in your body, what emotions do you think you are feeling?

Make a practice of checking in with your feelings

Practice checking in with your feelings several times a day At least once daily. The best times are when you get up in the morning and when you go to bed. You can best do it anywhere alone in a given space.

i. Take a few minutes to centre yourself. Take some deep breaths a and clear your mind of any thoughts. Go inside yourself and ask yourself "what am I feeling?" For simplicity sake, check for the following emotions: anger, sadness, fear, guilt, shame.

ii. Start by asking yourself "am I feeling angry?" Check in yourself and allow any angry feelings you might have to surface. If the answer is yes, simply list(in your head, out loud or on paper) the reasons you are feeling this way. For example, "I am angry that_____." Or Iam angry because_____."If the answer" no" proceed to the next emotion.

iii. Now ask yourself, " am I feeling sad?" Again, allow the feelings of sadness to bubble up and list all the reasons you feel sad.

iv. The next question is "am I feeling afraid?" Allow the feelings of fear to come up if they are there. If they are not, go on to the next feeling.

v. You do not need to do anything about the feelings that

have surfaced. The point of the check in is to help you to keep in touch with your feelings.

Connect your feelings with your needs

i. Check in with yourself several times a day by going inside and asking yourself what you are feeling.

ii. When you find a feeling, look for the corresponding need. Ask yourself "what do I need?" Often the answer will be, " feel my feeling and let it fade". Answer in the simplest way instead. For eg. If you are hungry you need food. When you are guilty, you need to apologize.

iii. It may take trying on several needs before you find the one that is true for you. You may also have many needs attached to one feeling. For eg. If you feel lonely your need may be to call a friend, to get a hug from your partner, to connect with yourself.

iv. Be on the alert for answers that are not only responding to you. For eg. "I feel sad, therefore, I need so a candy" or "I feel angry so I need to hit him" Tap into your inherent wisdom and relax into a more logical, self-nurturing answer. Ask yourself "okay, what do I really need?" For eg. "Express myself (write/sing a song). Get physical activity (walk, cycle), develop a plan, learn from it.

Stop treating yourself the way your parents treated you

Many nice girls deprive, abandon ,control, shame or ignore themselves just as their parents did to them. You may be so used to being deprived that you continue to deprive yourself. You may be so used to being ignored that you ignore self-care.

i. Make a list of the ways you neglect or deprive yourself of what you need.

ii. Write down every example you can think of regarding how your parents neglected to take care of you, include ways they deprived you emotionally as well as physically.

iii. Take a close look at your list and see if there is a connection between the way you treat yourself today and how you were treated by your parents.

Δ You don't have to stay trapped in repeating the depriving behaviour you learned from parents. You can become the responsive, nurturing and caring parent to yourself as you deserve all this while.

Discover what focussing on others does for you today

Payoffs to focussing outside of yourself

i. Take some time to think about what you get out of focussing on others more than yourself or to the exclusion of yourself. for eg. one answer that may come to you is that it's just a habit. That is a valid answer but try to dig a bit deeper to find some actual payoffs --specific benefits that you experience when you focus outside of yourself.

ii. Make a list of the reasons that you come up with. This may be difficult at first but keep working on it until you come up with some answers.

iii. Now I invite you to go deeper to examine the benefits of focussing on the needs and feelings of others or for your caretaking behaviour. Here is why it's written as follows:

Δ I realize that I feel good when I help others and gives me a sense of superiority

Δ I also feel that it diverts my attention away from myself and my inner critic that constantly makes me feel small of myself giving me a break from my negative self-talk.

Δ I somehow need to to justify my existence and I do this by helping others. I have self-doubt and many buried negative emotions so I help others to take the attention away of myself.

Start giving to yourself what you give to others

i. Make a list of all the things you do for those you love, especially acts of and nurturing. Do the things for yourself which you were doing benefiting others a good self-massage, eat a good meal, serve yourself save money, earn more, use your talents and beauty for money.

ii. Now list the reasons for your doing these things for eg. to satisfy your nagging mother, out of fear, to gain approval from her/others.

iii. Go over your list and think of similar ways you can nurture and take care of yourself. In the previous examples, the answers might be, "I need to think of reasons to be proud of myself and allow myself to feel that pride." It really raises my spirits everytime I look at my nails. I need to give myself the gift of having an appointment every week."

Δ Note that if you are involved with an abusive partner, there is something you need to understand: abusive people insist that their partners focus on their needs. The main way out of the abusive cycle is for you to reorient your thinking so that you devote your attention to yourself and your children. You need to stop trying to appease the abuser and turn your energy towards yourself.

Think of your need to focus on others as an addiction

One reason it is so difficult to give up focussing on others needs and feelings is that helping others can result immediate rewards. People respond positively to those who are kind, considerate and selfless. They show their appreciation by smiling at you, thanking you telling you what a wonderful caring person you are. It also feels good to do things for other people. It lands up into being resentful. Like giving up any addiction, it's going to be difficult to stop putting up other people's feelings and needs first. It has become automatic for you to put yourself last. That is why you need to create a routine, a practice of meeting your own needs. The more you repeat this new pattern, the more likely, it too will become automatic. The habit of doing daily or even hourly "feelings checking in" is a good practice to start.

Make a commitment to begin meeting your needs

Often in order for us to take action needed to create, a real change in our lives we need to make a commitment. This commitment needs to be a promise we make to ourselves not to anyone else that we will do something no matter what we can't put it off, we can't make excuses for not doing it we are committed to doing it.

i. Start by thinking about what you wanted from your parents but didn't receive. For eg. did you want their, encouragement? Their approval? Did you crave for more affection? Make a list of all the things you wished you had received from your parents but didn't get.

ii. List the ways you plan to start giving to to yourself what your parents didn't give to you. For eg. if you didn't receive encouragement, write on your list that you will begin to encourage yourself.

iii. Make a commitment to immediately begin doing one concrete thing that will provide you what you missed as a child.

As you see, many remedies have been listed in this chapter because learning to put your needs ahead of others needs is one of the most difficult habits for nice girls to break. You may not need every remedy listed, but take your time and address each remedy that applies to you.

Create a positive and powerful statement

"I have an obligation to myself and to others to take care of my own needs first".

Take a deep breath and take the words into your body, mind and spirit as you keep repeating this positive and powerful statement several times a day.

"I will remove toxic, selfish and evil people out of my life, and replace them with genuine respectful people who care for my well-being. I will nourish these new relationships and watch myself grow." Repeat this affirmation three times a day.

"I trust that my angels and spirit guides are sending me with tooth fairies and positive, loving people who care and fend for my wants and needs and I watch myself nourishing, growing and cheerful day by day". Visualize this affirmation and repeat every morning after waking up and best time before going to bed.

Discover or rediscover what your needs are

Our basic needs:
Take a close look at the following list of basic needs and think about how often you satisfy these needs for yourself.

Hunger- Give yourself healthy food to eat

Thirst - Give yourself plenty of water , not diet or soft drinks

Sleep- Go to bed early, don't eat before nor take stimulants

Companionship- Don't allow yourself to become isolated and reach out when you feel lonely

Sex- Provide yourself with healthy men for sex, neither depriving nor indulging for sex.

Stimulation- Get involved in activities that stimulates your mind, body and spirit

Spiritual connection- Get/satisfy your need for contemplation gratitude, prayer, ritual or any other type of expression you need.

Make a list of the needs you are meeting and how you are meeting them.

List the needs that have gone unmet and think of ways that you can begin to meet them.

Make the connection between needs and feelings

One way of discovering what your needs are at any given time is to check in with your feelings. Your feelings will tell you what you are lacking if you pay close attention. This may be a direct result of focussing on the feelings of others or having means of surviving childhood experiences such as neglect and trauma. Because of this you may experience a humble of feelings that you have difficulty identifying or as an adult be numb of your feelings. Therefore it is best to focus only on primary emotions anger, sorrow, joy, surprise, fear, discuss, guilt, shame, etc. The best way to discover your emotions are by asking yourself which ones you are experiencing at intervals during the day. It is safe to say that at any given time, we are all experiencing at least one or more of these.

Reconnect with your body

Just asking yourself which feeling you are experiencing won't necessarily help, if you aren't in touch with your body. Your body is the best barometer to tell you which emotion you are feeling at any given time. Emotions involve body changes, such as frustrations in heart rate and skin temperature and the tensing or relaxing muscles. Research as now think that changes in the facial muscles play an important role in actually causing emotions. For eg. we tend to feel sadness in our body in the following ways. Frowning or a slumped, hunched posture using a low tone of voice or swallowing in the throath sadness from holding back tears. Low on energy, feeling lethargic, listless wanting to stay in bed all day, feeling as though nothing is pleasurable anymore, feeling a pain or hollowness in your chest or gut feeling empty. Smiling feeling excited in the following ways alive active, glowing up or open hearted etc.

Reflection by examining your conscience

Take a moment to reflect upon and pen it down:

i. What changes do you need to make in your life?

ii. What have you had enough of?

iii. And will you commit to all that is necessary to acquire the changes you desire?

iv. How does the ideal life look to you?

v. What is your day filled with?

vi. How much time would you spend working and how much time would you have to relax?

vii. What would you do to achieve a state of calm and balance?

viii. Write down the people in your life that treated you badly...all

Δ People that you have chosen who are treating you badly and need to go

Δ People that are placed in your life , parents,siblings etc. in family. You need to limit contact with as much as possible. If you feel like you can shift environment for some through adjustments

Ask yourself these questions and give yourself time to come up with true answers that come from the heart.

Conclusion

'A Narc free World' is a life meaningful and purposeful away from clutter. The air is fresh to breathe the grass is greener on the outside and the surroundings more cleaner. And our lives are more magical with healthy loving people surrounding all through our lives. But God has destined us and we learn through trials and tests as those people who that trigger us teach us the most. We carry all the lessons that has been taught to us as it gives a lot of meaning in life. Though we learn lessons even from our enemies. Some people come in our life to use and abuse us, some to teach us, and some to bring out the best in us. In the law of mirroring, we learn from all our relationships. All we have to do is to bring in all the pieces together and complete the zig zag puzzle in our world by putting all the missing pieces back together to live a whole complete life.

Made in the USA
Monee, IL
07 March 2026

45640924R00038